C000133814

THE
Archive Photographs
SERIES
AROUND
BEBINGTON

This view of Higher Bebington Windmill was taken in 1897.

THE
Archive Photographs
SERIES
AROUND
BEBINGTON

Compiled by
Pat O'Brien

CHALFORD

First published 1995
Copyright © Pat O'Brien, 1995

The Chalford Publishing Company
St Mary's Mill, Chalford,
Stroud, Gloucestershire, GL6 8NX

ISBN 0 7524 0121 1

Typesetting and origination by
The Chalford Publishing Company
Printed in Great Britain by
Redwood Books, Trowbridge

The Bromborough to New Ferry horse-bus awaiting passengers at the terminus in New Ferry. The advertisement on the steps reads: 'MacDonald's Teeth'. This photograph is part of a multi-view postcard.

Contents

The Pier from Hotel, New Ferry

This view of the pier is dated 20 May 1905. It shows the old pier, which had to be closed on 3 April 1911 because it was badly in need of repair. A new stage was fitted, and its services resumed on 31 May.

Introduction

This book is an attempt to present a social history of the Bebington area in a pictorial form. It shows the days when the horse-bus was public transport, and 'Shank's pony' its alternative, and when Bromborough Pool Village and Port Sunlight were taking shape. It contains bygone scenes of our industrial heritage, and charts the changes that were taking place in public transport. Take a peep into these times of old, and you have the essence of local history.

When Bebington became a borough in 1937 it united surrounding villages and hamlets, each with its own identity and history which ranged from entries in *Domesday Book* to the foundation of Port Sunlight in 1888. With the aid of old photographs and postcards, a visual social history has been constructed which complements the various written works and preserves a visual record for posterity.

Because of the nature of the area, the range of topics to be covered is vast. They include ancient watermills, rural customs, maritime and transport history and scenes of early manufacturing, from candles to soap. Some of the local photographers were F. Walker of Little Sutton; George Davies (see page 159) and his son of New Chester Road; New Ferry (see page 155); W.J. McCullock,

Rock Ferry, and Lever Bros, who issued many views of Port Sunlight.

Eastham is listed in *Domesday Book*. At that time an extensive area of Wirral was included in its manor, making it the most important village in Wirral. Bromborough is an Anglo-Saxon place name; it is known that in 912 King Alfred's daughter established a monastery here. Bromborough also has a strong claim to be the site of the Battle of Brunaburh in 937. The first written record of the name Bebington appears in a charter of 1090, which confirms that it was granted, with Poulton, to Robert de Lancelyn. Spital, Raby, and Thornton Hough, all ancient settlements, have had their share of history too.

The history of Port Sunlight has been well recorded since its inception, and the photographs selected for this book show something of its architectural splendours and industrial development. Bromborough Pool Village, created in 1854, can lay claim to being the first industrial village in England. By 1858 the village contained seventy-six houses, a school, a cricket pavilion, and a bowling green. It expanded in stages thanks to the prosperity of the company that founded it – Prices Patent Candle Company Ltd. Last but not least is New Ferry, its ferry is sadly long gone, but its maritime history is recorded here in many evocative nautical pictures.

One
Eastham

This postcard was produced by F. Walker, Little Sutton. He probably got the children to pose for the photograph.

On 2 December 1887 the first steam navvy set to work on Eastham Locks. It removed soil at the rate of 1200 cubic yards a day, and kept 700 men fully occupied.

Much progress has been made: the banks have been shaped, and the bed of the canal is in the final stages of being levelled out. In the distance Stanlow Point can be seen protruding into the estuary.

The three locks were constructed inside the protection of a huge embankment. In September 1890 a dredger, the *Manchester*, started to cut its way in from the estuary to the site of the lock gates.

A huge shed was constructed at Eastham in which the lock gates were built. They were made of greenheart wood; this tree, which comes from British Guiana, is a hard wood which will sink in water and is impervious to insects.

GENERAL VIEW OF THE EASTHAM
LOCKS CLEARED FOR THE
ADMISSION OF THE WATER.

A general view of the Eastham Locks, cleared for the admission of water.

Once the lock gates had been installed, the outer dam was demolished. By the first week of June 1891 the way from the channel in the Sloyne to the outer lock was clear.

The first vessel to enter the locks was the Norseman. Her owner was Mr Samuel Platt. Mr Leader Williams was the Manchester Ship Canal engineer.

The Royal Yacht *Enchantress* arriving at Eastham on Monday 21 May 1894 after being at Salford Docks to participate in the opening of the Manchester Ship Canal by Queen Victoria.

There are three sea locks, measuring 600 feet by 80 feet, 350 feet by 50 feet, and 150 feet by 30 feet. To the north (estuary end) of the locks are storm gates, which were constructed to open outwards and intended to be closed for protection when north westerly winds accompanied high spring tides.

At Eastham Locks there was a dismantling crane and wharf which removed and stored masts and funnel tops which were too high to pass beneath the bridges on the way to Salford Docks.

These four postcard views were taken c. 1912–13 (see below), and show in sequence how a large ship was brought into Eastham Locks accompanied by tugs, and afterwards guided up the Manchester Ship Canal.

Eastham Locks.

Two sets of locks are paired: the larger, 600-foot one, and the smaller, 350-foot one. The value of the paired locks is fully realised when a large ship accompanied with its tugs approaches the entrance. This view is dated 7 July 1913.

Eastham Locks.

The ship enters the larger lock and the tugs the smaller; thus they are ready and waiting when the ship enters the canal.

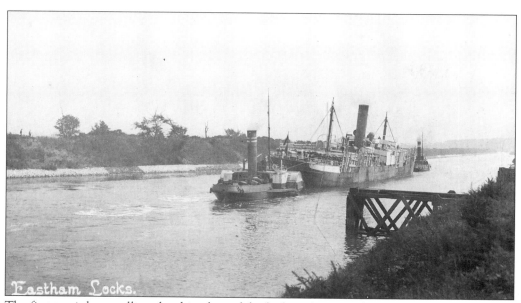

Eastham Locks.

The first tug is busy pulling the ship clear of the lock so the second tug can take up its position at the rear. Then, between them, they can guide it up the canal. Note the old paddle-wheeler type of tug boat.

This floating jetty was the last landing stage to be used at Eastham. The ferry can be identified as the *Ruby* because it had a much longer white band painted on its funnel. Compare this to the other boats.

The *Ruby* was built in 1897 by J. Jones of Liverpool. It had 171 gross tonnage, a length of 124 feet, a width of 22 feet, and a depth of 8 feet, making it the smallest of these three boats. The boats were painted in the company colours of blue and white, the amount of white varying with each boat. The ferry service closed down in 1929.

The *Sapphire* was built in 1898, also by J. Jones of Liverpool. Its length was 140 feet, breadth 24 feet, depth 8 feet and it was 223 gross tonnage, making it the largest of the three boats.

The *Pearl* was 171 gross tonnage, and was built by J. Jones of Liverpool. Its length was 130 feet, breadth 22 feet, and depth 8 feet. Like the *Ruby* and the *Sapphire*, it was a paddle steamer, and had new boilers installed in 1812. It was owned by The New Liverpool and Eastham Hotel Company.

As one stepped off the ferry boat, to the left was the old sandstone ticket office where one obtained tickets. The building is still used, now for other purposes. The Eastham Ferry Hotel, in the background, no longer has its magnificent verandah.

The jubilee arch that stood at the entrance to the Pleasure Gardens is said to have been built and originally erected in Liverpool, but because it obstructed local development it was taken down and relocated here.

In the summer months the gardens were a hive of activity with non-stop entertainment. There was a menagerie, band concerts, circus acts, and many other attractions. For those who wanted a quiet walk, there were the flower gardens.

The Fair Ground, Eastham Ferry.

For the children, the main attraction had to be the fairground with its swingboats, hobby horses, and its famous loop-de-loop ride. The fairground owner was known to all as Aunt Polly. Was she the same 'Polly' as the postmistress on page 35?

23

Opposite the two young men and outside the ferry ticket office was the stand for the horse taxi service to the village. At busy periods the taxi would transport people up to the village and St Mary's Church, or from there to the pleasure gardens or the ferry.

Some of the tea rooms along the Ferry Road: W.C. Pearson, 'school treats specially catered for' with a 'private field for sports', and the Hankinson, late Johnson refreshment room, which offered roast beef or lamb with a choice of vegetables for 1s 3d.

Looking up Ferry Road towards the village of Eastham on a quiet day. Note the contrast with the same scene below, which looks down the road.

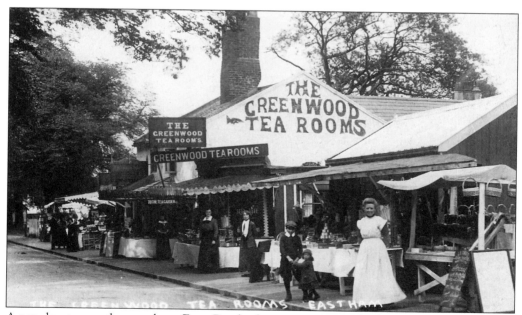

A popular stop on the way down Ferry Road, where cream teas and other refreshments could be taken, was the Greenwood Tea Rooms. Mrs Jessie O'Brien is seen outside the Tea Rooms, which she owned from c. 1910 until the 1930s.

Canon Torr was born in Carlett Park and baptised in Eastham Church on 10 October 1851. He married Julia Elizabeth Holmes in 1878 and they had seven children: five girls and two boys. He was inducted as vicar of Eastham in August 1880 and carried out his duties for the next thirty-seven years, until he resigned on 2 February 1917.

Shown clearly here is the 'broach' spire of St. Mary's, one of only two such spires in Wirral. The other one is at St Barnabas, Bromborough. A broach spire is one that 'drips' over a parapet, and seems unsupported.

This ceremonial arch was erected in Eastham village as part of the wedding celebrations when Katherine Ann Torr married Charles Bushell in 1871. She was a sister to Canon W.E. Torr.

Canon Torr proudly escorts his daughter Sybil and her entourage of bridesmaids towards the entrance of St Mary's Church on the occasion of her wedding on 1 August 1907. The crowds on either side are mainly of ladies eager to get a close-up view of the beautiful wedding clothes worn by the bride and her bridesmaids.

The streets of Eastham were decorated for the wedding.

MISS TORR'S WEDDING DAY AT EASTHAM CHURCH
THE BRIDE BEING ESCORTED TO THE CHURCH BY HER BROTHER

This is Gertrude Louisa Torr being escorted to St Mary's Church for her wedding to the Revd C.J. Holmes on 30 July 1912, by one of her two brothers.

The official wedding group taken after the ceremony on 30 July. Most such photographs were sold as postcards, so that local people could have mementoes of local events.

Set against the background of her home, Carlett Park, the reception following Miss Torr's wedding on 30 July 1912 is taking place. The string quartet play popular tunes while close friends mingle, or enjoy a tête-à-tête.

A close-up of the same wedding reception shows some of the more elderly guests partaking of refreshments at tables on the lawns in front of Carlett Park.

This is Gersham Stewart, Member of Parliament for Wirral, paying an official visit to Eastham to thank his supporters after being elected in 1910.

All the important local events were photographed. This shows Empire Day at Eastham Show, 24 May 1910.

Coronation Day at Eastham, 22 June 1911. Celebrations like this took place throughout the land.

After its construction Eastham Locks was a popular attraction with locals and visitors alike. They would stroll up from the ferry and along the river bank, gazing at the hive of activity the locks created.

This charming study is of the maypole dance at Eastham on 1 July 1911.

On the left is the old village post office and on the far corner is the ancient Hooton Arms, alongside the road leading to the ferry.

Eastham Mill was a small eighteenth-century tower windmill situated outside the village, to the south. It was operational until 1895. Millers included William Crabb (until 1870); his son William (until 1892); and then William Spark (also in the early 1890s).

Down at Eastham Locks the maritime fraternity had its own post office. The local postmistress was known to everyone as 'Polly'.

This is a group of former pupils of the Church School. They are pictured with Canon Torr; the head teacher, Mr Allan; and a former teacher, Mr Reg Davies, now in uniform and about to depart for the battlefields of Europe.

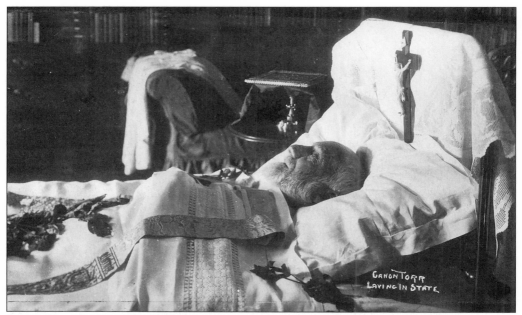

Canon Torr died on 17 September 1924, and in accordance with the custom of the times his body was laid out in state. Dressed in his ecclesiastical vestments, he was laid out on his bed at Carlett Park so that his parishioners could come and pay their last respects.

After lying in state, the body was cremated. At this time not many people were cremated and it was certainly rare for a member of the clergy.

Here, the casket containing the ashes of the late Canon Torr, covered with flowers, is being carried into the church for the funeral service. The bier was carried by Messrs Elliot, Duncan, Davies, and Ward (senior).

After the service, the ashes were placed in the grave of his wife and his daughter Lilian Hope Torr, who died as a baby in 1884.

This is the dedication of the village's First World War memorial. There are thirty-five names inscribed on it – a large number for such a small community.

Plymyard House was constructed on the site of a monastic grange (farm) belonging to the Abbey of St Werburgs at Chester. Although this building was demolished in 1976, part of the ancient grange still exists as a section of a private house not far away. Part of the monastery's bakehouse can be seen on an outer wall, and underneath the house is a medieval well which supplied water to the grange.

Two
Around Bromborough

This is the New Ferry-Bromborough omnibus. The service was started in 1898 by the Wirral Tramway Co. as an extension of their tram route from Woodside. It had several owners before being taken over in 1902 by Oxon Carriage Co. Ltd. The company's initials can be seen on the driver's apron.

The late Mrs Anne Anderson on her 87th birthday in 1969. A historian and an author, Mrs Sanderson was one of the founder members of the Bromborough Society, inaugurated in 1933 and still going strong. Their motto, 'Hold fast that which is good', is one that members still live up to.

Originally called Spann's Tenement, but now known as Stanhope House, this building dating from 1693 is Wirral's finest example of a seventeenth-century merchant's house. It is still with us today owing to the valiant efforts of the Bromborough Society, who saved it from destruction.

The parish church of St Barnabas is the third church to have stood on this site. The present church was built in 1863–4 on a site south-west of the Saxon church site. The Lord of the Manor, Salusbury K. Mainwaring, laid the foundation stone.

Here we have the shop of F. Davies, 'Wholesale & Retail, Corn, Flour, Bread & Provender Merchants'. The shop was situated on the old Chester Road. In the *Morris Directory of Cheshire* for 1874, Richard and Ellis Davies are listed as bakers.

As the hostilities of the First World War came to an end, peace was celebrated in various ways throughout the country. Here, the people of Bromborough are gathered around the village cross, while local dignitaries express their thanks.

42

'White Row' stood on the east side of what was once the main road from Chester. Some of the houses were occupied by families employed at nearby Bromborough Hall.

This view, dated 28 August 1906, is important because it shows the site of the Bromborough smithy. The noticeboard advertises the blacksmith shop of L. Sheridan, the village blacksmith. See the chapter on Bebington for a photograph of the other forge owned by the same family.

This is the south side of the Rake, looking west. The word 'Rake', used in a number of Wirral place-names, means either a principal lane or a boundary between two places.

The Rake looking east, with Carling's shop selling confectionery and tobacco and other provisions. The finger post points the way of the public footpath to Woodchurch.

Behind the wall on the right stood Bromborough Hall (see page 47), the home of the Mainwaring family. The road is the old Chester Road, which was once a turnpike.

At the corner of Allport Lane in 1906. There are two shops: J. Clover, and Whiteways the butchers. Across the road the wooden building situated next to Tellet's farmhouse carries an advertisement for Spratt's Dog Food.

This is the elite section of the spectators who attended who attended the Sunday Schools Sports at Bromborough. This was known as the 'half-a-crown side', and chairs were provided. The event probably took place in the grounds of Bromborough Hall.

This photograph of a group of Bromborough Boy Scouts is reputed to have been taken before 1914.

The original hall was once a palace for the Bishops of Chester. After passing through various owners it came into the Mainwaring family, who later became Lords of Bromborough. The house was demolished in 1932 to make way for a bypass.

Bromborough Juniors Football Club proudly display their trophy. The date is not known.

The Royal George, seen here near the Bromborough Arms in Bromborough village, was the first Crosville bus to operate on the New Ferry to Chester service (see page 151).

This is the other side of the Bromborough Hotel. The boundary wall on the left belongs to Bromborough Hall, whose extensive parklands stretched down as far as the estuary shoreline.

As the village expanded, both sides of the New Chester Road were gradually developed for housing, which reached all the way to Bromborough Pool Bridge.

Station Road was once the name given to this part of Allport Lane.

The brook spanned by the bridge is called the Dibbin, from which the dale gets its name. Originally called Poultondale, from 1839 onwards it became known as Dibbinsdale.

The road runs parallel to the valley and the brook, which runs down to the Mersey estuary via Bromborough Pool.

Spital Road. The origin of the name refers to the leper house (or hospital) which was recorded in the Chartulary of the Abbey of St Werburgs between 1270 and 1283. The hospital site was at Spittle Old Hall.

The village of Spital was part of the manor of Poulton Hall.

Before the construction of the dock gates at Bromborough Dock, this area stood near the highest point, its position chosen to avoid the thirty-foot spring tides.

The Dibbin divided here around a section of marshland known as Wharf Island. A weir blocked the western side, and the mill was built on the narrowest part of the eastern side.

THE DAM and OLD MILL SITE, BROMBOROUGH

A watermill was recorded in *Domesday Book* for this area, and was later mentioned again in a Chartulary of St Werburgs Abbey, Chester, in 1398. The site was Wharf Island (see page 52).

To supplement water power a windmill was built in 1777 and it operated until 1878, when it was found to be unsafe and blown up. From 1835, steam had also been used as an additional source of power to the water mill.

The engine house, built of red sandstone, and the tall brick chimney date from 1835, when a Liverpool firm, Fawcett, Preston & Co. Ltd, were involved in the conversion.

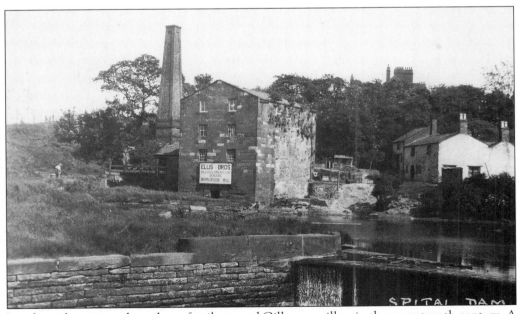

Local parish registers show that a family named Gill were millers in the seventeenth century. A local family named Ellis received the water mill in 1777 by indenture, and held it until 1959, when it was demolished.

Three
Raby and Thornton Hough

About a mile and a half from Bromborough lies the village of Raby, with its famous man-made mere, which was created as a storage pond for the local water mill.

The Wheatsheaf has been an inn for over 350 years; the landlord in the 1861 Trade Directory was William Ellison. In 1891 it was a freehouse owned by the Earl of Shrewsbury, and according to the *Register of Licensed Houses* it had one bed for travellers and catering facilities for ten people.

Close by the tea gardens is another much-visited beauty spot, the stepping stones.

The road shown here was also the mill dam. The mill was situated below the level of the then mill pond, and when water was required to operate the wheel it was sent down under control.

The Mere is nearly a quarter of a mile in length and surrounded by woods which reach down to the water's edge. The dam can be seen in the previous view. The boats for hire on the mere belonged to the Williamson family.

The mill wheel shown on the right is known as an 'overshot' type, by which the water would fall on top of the wheel (12 o'clock) and the water power would then drive the wheel full circle. Millers are recorded as working here from 1726; the Williamson family were millers from 1869 to 1892.

The earliest dates to have been found on the old mill building are 1601 and 1704, and the mere must have been created sometime in the seventeenth or early eighteenth century to act as a storage for the water power.

When the mill was no longer used for grinding corn, a firm of metal merchants, Collins of Birkenhead, used to bring cartloads of files to be ground by water power.

When the mill ceased working, the mill house and surrounding area were converted into a tea garden establishment.

The tea garden is run by the Williamson family, who are descended from the milling family of the same name. This was an official correspondence card used by them, which advertised the tea garden at the same time.

In Thornton Hough there are two churches – the parish church and the Congregational church. Through the munificence of Mr J. Hirst, the church, the vicarage, and the schools were built in 1866–68. This church has a five-faced clock, so that Mr Hirst could see it from his bedroom window.

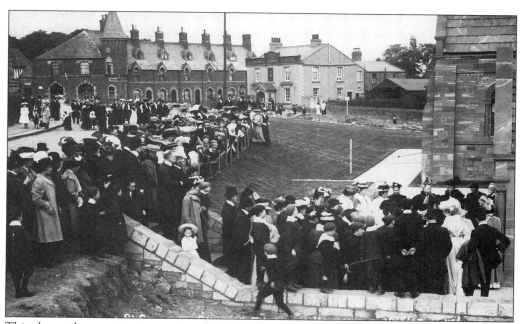

This shows the opening ceremony of St George's Congregational Church by Mr Lever on 29 May 1907. Executed in the purest Norman style, it is said to be unique in England. It is the loveliest modern church in Wirral.

The original Thornton Manor was built in the 1840s, and in 1888 Mr William Lever, later to become the First Viscount Leverhulme, occupied it as a tenant. In 1891 he purchased the property from its owner, Sir Thomas Forwood.

He then started to alter the house and redesign the gardens completely. The alterations were completed by 1914 and very little now remains of the original buildings. Much magnificent furniture and many works of art were displayed here before the Lady Lever Art Gallery was built.

Each year, children from Port Sunlight went on a picnic to Thornton Manor. At the entrance gate the Levers would greet each child and give them a book of tickets which gave them a turn at the coconut shy, a roundabout ride, and a boat trip on the lake. There was a picnic tea in a bag and a packet of toffees to take home.

When Viscount Lever came to live at Thornton Manor, he decided to build a model village for his estate workers similar to Port Sunlight.

This shows the extent of the private lake within the grounds of Thornton Manor. Surrounded by trees, it is sheltered from the elements and the gaze of the general public.

Boating on the lake attached to the Manor was not just reserved for friends of the family. Local groups, including the Boy Scouts, were invited to use it and its facilities.

Four
Lower and
Higher Bebington

Bromborough Road, Bebington. Nº. A1.

Until the new turnpike road (New Chester Road) was built, with its toll houses and gates at Bromborough and New Ferry, this was the main road.

This old inn was on the main road to the ferries. As many as thirty coaches a day passed along this way; in those days inns and alehouses along the route 'captured the passing trade', and the Gladstone Arms was no exception. When the village was bypassed, this inn was not the only casualty.

Kirket Lane derived its name from its route to the church (kirk) gate. It is also known as the 'Roman road' although there is no evidence of a Roman road here. The nearest one, stretching from Chester's Northgate, has been traced through Great Sutton and Willaston, heading towards Meols.

St. Andrew's, Lower Bebington, is one of the finest old parish churches in Wirral. Although it has undergone extensive alterations, it exhibits a vast range of architectural styles. The saltire cross of St Andrew's is a prominent feature in the Borough coat of arms.

Because of overcrowding in the churchyards, local Boards of Health in 1850 were given the power to provide cemeteries. Situated in Town Lane, this cemetery was created in 1868; it consisted of 22½ acres which were landscaped at a cost of £17,900. There were three mortuary chapels for Anglicans, Nonconformists, and Catholics respectively.

Church Road, looking up the hill with St Andrew's churchyard on the left. A large housing estate has replaced a lot of private property that once stood here except, of course, Edgeworth (see page 72).

The shops of yesteryear: G.M. Patterson; Moody's wine merchants; Scotts bread and confectionery; and Appletons household stores.

Looking towards Lower Bebington. The postman appears to have posed for the photographer – does anyone know anything about him?

The 'Thatched Cottage', built in 1653, clad in an overcoat of snow. It is still with us – rural heritage at its best.

This procession through Lower Bebington forms part of the celebration commemorating the coronation of King George V.

This is Acres Road; the building at the corner was originally the old Dog & Gun, later the old post office. The building is now occupied by F.R. Kirk & Son, Undertakers. More festivities celebrating the coronation of King George V.

This is a photograph of Lottie Dodd, aged nine years. In 1887, at the age of fifteen years, she won the Wimbledon Ladies' title. She was also a golf champion, played hockey and won a silver medal for archery in the Olympic Games of 1908.

This is Edgeworth, Lottie's parental home in the 1880s. The house, with its tennis court, was situated in Church Road. Born in 1871, she died in 1960.

This shows Lottie Dodd captaining the North Hockey Team which beat the South Hockey Team 6-2 in February 1900. Lottie is seen sitting down holding the ball.

Lottie Dodd is seen here competing in the Archery section of the Olympic Games on 17 July 1908, where she won the Archery Silver Medal.

This is the Bebington Cycling Club meeting outside the Brown Cow Vaults before the start of one of their cycling tours. This picture was taken c. 1900.

Bebington Football Club in 1921, better known to their supporters as the 'Lily Whites'. I wonder why?

The Wirral Farmer's Club was inaugurated by Charles Stanley of Denhall, near Neston. It later became the Birkenhead & Wirral Agricultural Society, and during its early years it held shows in various parts of Wirral until it found a permanent showground in Bebington.

Every type of farming livestock can be seen here, from the Grand Parade of bulls in the foreground to the working horses dressed up in their finery and jingling brasses, and the shire horses in the background. The posters are advertising the Royal Lancashire Show in Liverpool.

B'HEAD SHOW —

The grounds were used as an army camp in the First World War, and after that war the show never resumed. The land was then bought for a sports ground by Levers, and it became known as The Oval. Later still, it was bought for use by local schools.

The Princess Royal being introduced to the officers of various youth groups by the Mayor of Bebington at Bebington Youth Rally held at The Oval in 1944.

In the distance can be seen the side wall of the Dog & Gun with its large painted sign advertising its wares, a relic from the days when it was a pub.

Taken in 1904, this picture shows the Dog & Gun during its last days as a public house.

In this picture the wall sign has been obliterated, showing it is no longer a pub. On the right, the furthest building bears a notice which reads, 'C.H. Carpenter, Car Proprietor, Livery & Bait Stables'.

This photograph was taken on 3 September 1913. The large plaque between the two upstairs windows used to be the 'Dog and Gun' nameplate. During this period it was a general store on the left, and the Bebington Post Office on the right.

This group of cottages was known as Trafalgar. They were built to house Storeton quarry workers and the name was given after Nelson's victory.

The Sheridans were a well-known local family of blacksmiths. One smithy was located in Bromborough (see page 43), and this is the other one in Lower Bebington.

The foundation stone was laid on 1 August 1857, the fabric being consecrated on 24 December 1859. In 1879 a parish was assigned to it, comprising the portion of this township lying above the old Chester Road.

This is what the village of Higher Bebington used to look like.

This is Village Road, Higher Bebington, in 1902. The whitewashed cottage at the bottom of the road stood at the corner of King's Brow.

This is Mount Road at the corner of Bracken Lane and Red Hill Road. The Wishing Gate was a well-known spot, where courting couples would stand on either side of the gate and then, joining their hands through the bars, make a wish.

The sails on Bebington Mill date this picture to before the First World War. In addition to the horse-drawn tram, a steam engine called *Storeton* was used on the tram track as far as Bebington Station. It fetched down stone to be used when the main railway line was increased from two to four tracks, between 1902 and 1904.

The end wall, supported by massive buttresses, once formed part of the ancient Storeton Hall. The pointed window frame of the chapel can be seen, blocked in. Other remains form part of the barns and stables. The hall was replaced by a substantial farmhouse.

These are the footprints of a prehistoric animal which was found sixty feet below the surface in Storeton Quarry. They measure eight inches by five inches, and are said to resemble a human hand. They can be seen in the Williamson Art Gallery.

Between 1925 and 1933 a lot of the material excavated from the workings of the Mersey Tunnel was used to fill in the quarries.

Built in the first part of the nineteenth century, the old windmill then belonged to Mr Lightbound. It was sold to Mr Johnson *c*. 1870, and then to Mr (later Alderman) Reg Williams in 1905. Alongside the mill is the metal chimney of a portable engine, the *Wirral Lassie*, which was used to drive the machinery on windless days. The engine was hired out to farms at harvest time to assist with threshing. It ceased working during January 1901, after the miller had some steam mills built in Birkenhead. Millers were W. Lightbound (1868), J.F. Lightbound (1874), S. Johnson (1892–96). The last miller was Mr H. Johnson, who died in 1947.

Until 1971 the windmill on Mill Brow overlooking Storeton Quarries was a landmark that could be seen from miles around.

The sails of Bebington Mill were taken down during the First World War and the buildings were used for storing machinery. The mill was demolished in 1971 and later on the land was developed for housing.

New Schools, Bebington .

The two New Schools in Higher Bebington took over five years to build. They were designed by the county's architect, Mr F. Anstead Browne. The boys' school was situated in Cross Lane, and the girls' school (above) in Heath Road. Both schools were officially opened on Saturday 26 September 1931 by Brigadier-General Sir William Bromley-Davenport. The title Bebington was changed to Wirral within a month, and in 1936 the schools' title became Wirral County Grammar Schools. One famous pupil at the boys' school was Harold Wilson, now Lord Rievaulx, Prime Minister from 1964 to 1970 and from 1974 to 1976.

The entire Wirral Grammar School for Boys, 1954. This is a continuous picture that runs from

top left to bottom right.

Wirral Grammar School for Boys, Form III, T2, 1956. Back row: B. Jenks, L. Dreaper, A. Ellis, G. Kent, D. Harrison, F. Waring, R. Jones, R. Smith, F. York, D. Hope, E. Barrat, B. Malcolm. Middle row: B. Sidebotham, A. van Beek, B. Collins, B. Bell, A. Freeman, S. Birch, E. Cooper, I. Wilson, D. Buckley, I. Ingham. Front row: D. Holmes, K. Davies, M. Thompson, B. Pritchard, L. Royds H. Povall (Big Bill), W. Williams, P. Shaw, M. Robinson, B. Edwards, G. Parry.

Wirral County Grammar School for Girls, 5th Form, 1961. Back row: Jean Hurst, Valerie Fannon, Ann Fleming, Ann Davies, Diane Pemberton, Anne McCorquedale, Lesley Laval, Sheila Topham, Hilary Marsh. Front row: Valerie Kirkham, Frances Collinson, Valerie Johnson, Jackie Holtham, Janet Curtis, Beryl A. Edkins (teacher), Jennifer Moss, Jill Timmis, Maureen Bestwick, Jennifer Kilner, Joan Davis.

During the night of 31 August 1940, the Wirral Grammar School for Boys was one of a number of buildings to be damaged in a bombing raid. This view was taken from inside the assembly hall.

Taken from the outside, this photograph shows the extensive damage to the school hall and room 1. This area was to remain a ruin for the next eleven years.

On the night of 12–13 March 1941 bombs were dropped on parts of Bebington. The collapsed house, Whispers, was in Thornton Road at the junction of Harley Avenue. It was later demolished and a new house, also called Whispers, was built on the site.

This shows the extensive bomb damage in Town Lane following the same raid.

Five
Port Sunlight

This is a bird's eye view of Port Sunlight works from Corniche Road. The water tower above No. 1 Soapery can be seen between the two chimney stacks (see p.95).

Barges would travel up the creek on a full tide and discharge their cargoes of raw materials near the melting-out sheds. This photograph shows barges being loaded with the finished product at the Wharf *c.* 1890.

By 1895 a new wharf had been completed to handle the ever-increasing supplies of raw materials needed to feed the manufacturing process. In the background is No. 1 Soapery. One of these barges was named *The Herald of Peace*. The photograph was taken *c.* 1900.

This is No. 1 Soapery, where the first boil of Sunlight Soap was made in mid-June 1889. Only the soap making buildings were permitted to rise above one storey in height. The water tower above No. 1 Soapery was a well-known landmark. The coal wagons belonged to the Wirral Colliery at Neston.

Each of these pans could hold up to sixty tons of materials. Caustic soda was added to blended vegetable oils and animal fats, and brought to the boil with steam. Here, for the first time, steam was injected into the materials; in the past, steam coils had been used.

This is the cooling room with its 800 cast iron frames where the soap mixture went solid. After several days of cooling down, the frames were removed and the blocks of soap were cut into slabs. They were later sliced into bars ready for stamping and packing.

Inside the stamping and wrapping room in No. 1 Soapery, bars of soap were cut into various sizes by a workforce constituted mainly of young women. Several young boys were used to carry out various menial tasks; here, they are under the watchful eye of their bearded foreman. This photograph was taken c. 1901.

This is a view of the stamping room, No. 1 Soapery, *c.* 1910. Two young women at the front of the photograph are using a rotary stamping machine. At the back, several young women can be seen packing Sunlight Soap.

Girls Packing Soap, Port Sunlight.

A busy scene in the packing room in 1912 shows girls busy packing bars of soap, including the famous 'Sunlight'.

Young women making cartons for Sunlight Soap in the Lever Bros. factory at Port Sunlight, 1910.

This young lady is packing Sunlight soap in the factory in 1910.

When shown a thin sheet of soap, Lever recalled the Lancashire housewives, standing over the dolly tub and cutting chips from a bar of soap for the Monday morning wash. Thus began the soapflake – first known as Sunlight and then, from 1900 onwards, as Lux.

This group of young ladies worked in Levers in the 1930s. Sadly, we know none of their names.

The printing room printed packages for the various products, and also the very popular *Sunlight Year Book* which was crammed with competitions and useful household tips. They also printed the *Sunlight Almanac* and posters of all shapes and sizes for advertising.

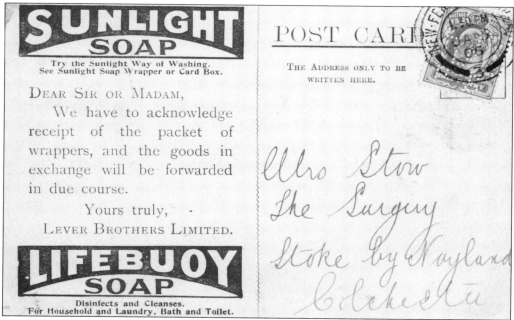

This official card from Levers is in acknowledgement of a special offer held in 1905. In the *Sunlight Year Book* of the 1890s there were many literary and photographic competitions, and prizes were offered for models made out of Sunlight Soap card boxes. There were also colouring competitions for the little ones.

When it was first formed, the voluntary Ambulance Corps consisted of twenty men and several women who received an extra shilling in their wage packet for this duty and another shilling 'per monthly drill'. When this picture was taken, in 1909, the group had expanded with the workforce.

This scene, showing members of staff entering the main entrance to the offices at Port Sunlight, was taken before the First World War.

Many of the attractive posters advertising Sunlight Soap on the roadside and railway station hoardings featured children and family pets, and other happy domestic scenes.

This is William Hesketh Lever, the founder of Port Sunlight. When he was granted a barony in 1917 he took the maiden name of his late wife, Elizabeth Hulme, to form the title Leverhulme. He was born in Bolton, Lancashire, in 1851, and died in London in 1925. This photograph was taken in 1901, when he was fifty years of age.

This is Victoria Bridge in the process of construction. Completed in 1897, it was opened in June 1898 by Mr Reid, the Premier of New South Wales. Its name commemorated the Diamond Jubilee of Queen Victoria. It was built to carry the Bolton Road over the widest tidal inlet from Bromborough Pool.

Dell, Corniche Road, Port Sunlight.

This was originally a tidal inlet between Corniche Road and Church Drive. Victoria Road spanned it, giving access to the New Chester Road.

Here is one of the narrow-gauge locomotives with wagon-loads of material excavated from the soap works construction site, seen here in Wood Street on its way to fill up some of the hollows in the village. The picture was taken in 1905.

These little trains were known as the 'Irish Expresses', but nobody knows why. This photograph shows driver John King in charge of Kerr-Stuart No. 1100, 2-feet gauge locomotive, one of the last 'Irish Expresses' to have been working in the village.

The filling in of the tidal inlets started in 1905. The narrow-gauge tracks seen here were laid and lifted as the work sites were moved. Notice the infill under Victoria Bridge here, and in the view below.

When the infill was low under the bridge, it was used as a target range for the Rifle Club. At the finish the infill level completely buried the bridge and the parapet used for the rail bridge on the New Chester Road.

Bolton Road could be termed as the main street; some of its houses were the first to be built, and a list of its occupants shows its importance. One was Edward Wainwright, Lever Bros' first soap boiler at their works in Warrington; other occupants were the minister, the doctor, and the schoolmaster.

This was the only area in which Lever had to demolish previous houses; these used to face the Pinfold and Almhouse on Primrose Hill. They were a group of overcrowded and tumbledown slums, and extant photographs show this clearly. These houses replaced them.

This started as a village shop in 1891. As the village required more shops, it became a post office (see page 110).

The Auditorium, Port Sunlight.

The auditorium was constructed as an open-air theatre in 1905, but because of consistent bad weather was soon given an iron frame to support a canvas covering. After conversion into a solid structure in 1906, it could accommodate 3000 spectators. It was also used as a skating rink for a time, and was demolished in 1937.

Girls' Institute, Port Sunlight.

This group of buildings went through several transformations. In 1894 it was turned into three shops run by company employees on co-operative lines. The first floor, above them, was built as a girls' institute, its emphasis more educational than social. Here the girls were taught cookery, dressmaking, shorthand, and other skills. A course of twelve lessons in any subject cost one shilling (supplemented by the firm).

Hulme Hall (Girls Dining Hall), Port Sunlight.

The hall was built in 1901 and took Mrs Lever's maiden name. It was built as a women's dining room, but as the works expanded it became too small for the number of women employed so a canteen was opened in the works. During the Second World War it was used as a billet for the American troops who dealt with American ammunition ships using Bromborough Docks.

110

William Hesketh Lever stood for Parliament four times before being elected as Liberal member for Wirral in 1906. Accompanied by brass bands, his workers gave him a rousing reception on his election.

This building served a dual purpose. It was used as an assembly and recreation hall while also serving as a men's dining hall until a canteen was provided in the factory in 1910. It was given its name, Gladstone Hall, because Mr Gladstone performed the opening ceremony.

Technical Institute, Port Sunlight.

The building of the Technical Institute started in 1902 and was completed in 1903. The cost was met by Lever himself, not by the company. The part of the building facing New Chester Road presents a dazzling display of seventeenth-century-style pargetting, a complete contrast to that which is shown here.

Employees were encouraged in all sporting activities. On the village site plans for 1910 two tennis lawn sites and bowling greens can be seen.

The open air swimming baths, built in 1902, were situated on the southern end of the Causeway and Queen Mary's Drive. On the left are the dressing huts, which were thatched. The facilities were also used by the nearby Wirral Grammar School for Boys; here, the boys were taught to swim and until its closure in 1971 they held their annual swimming gala here.

Village Schools. Park Road, Port Sunlight

This building, known today as the Lyceum, built between 1894 and 1896 and enlarged in 1898, was originally the school. Church services were also held here. The school was run by the company until the 1902 Education Act (see page 141).

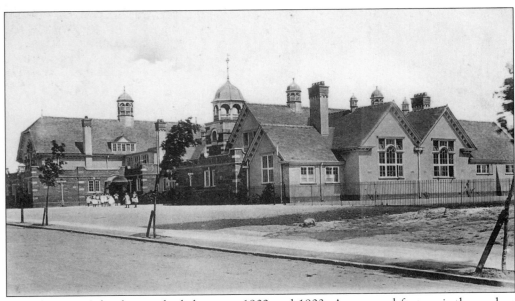

Church Drive Schools were built between 1902 and 1903. An unusual feature is the sunken playground which was created out of part of the main channel of the tidal inlet that used to be at the back of the building.

Church Drive School, Port Sunlight, 1907. Back row (left to right) are: F. Jebb, W. Beattie, F. Clow, G. Beech, G. Stanley, D. Middleton, -?- White. Second row from back: -?- Jones, -?- Watson, -?- Davies, -?- Furnival, -?- Repton, W. Burgess, D. Atkinson, L. Rock. Third row from back: H. Elliot, E. Denson, -?- Henry, -?- Embry, B. Bates, Headmaster Mr Simister, Fourth row from back: Teacher Miss Johnson, A. Scott, A. Purvis, G. Nicholson, D. Cribbon, J. Pierce, N. Hannon. Fifth row from back: W. Cawson, H. Cambridge, L. Turner, E. Taylor, B. Wooton, M. Jones, N. Sanderson. Front row: -?- Coulson, T. Jones, W. Patterson, J. Scott.

In its early days the factory had its own fire brigade of six men. They also took Lever's shilling for drills. The horse-drawn appliances were replaced in 1914 by motorised vehicles.

Because of the hazards of fire with raw materials, every department was provided with new inventions such as automatic fire alarms, and in the roofs there were automatic sprinklers, fed by tanks containing over four thousand gallons of water. This is a fire at No. 1 Oil Mill, 25 February 1926.

Each year, on the Sunday School anniversary, the children and their teachers would march through the village to the Auditorium. Lever considered these processions to be so important that on special occasions he and his family would march in front of the procession carrying the banner.

This is Port Sunlight School's Anniversary Procession, dated 3 July 1909, proceeding up Greendale Road. The writer of the postcard asks the addressee if he can be identified in the crowd of spectators.

Because there were over six hundred children attending the Sunday School – including those not old enough for infant school – there were eight Sunday Schools housed in different buildings. On the Sunday School Anniversary in 1909 they all assembled together in the Auditorium.

An observation saloon carriage was loaned to Lever Bros by Cambrian Railways for the royal visit of King George V and Queen Mary on 25 March 1914. It can be seen here, arriving at Port Sunlight station and entering the works via Lever's own railway network.

This commemorative medallion was issued to employees of Lever Bros on the occasion of the royal visit to Port Sunlight on 25 March.

Ladies' soccer teams have been recorded at Lever's since the 1914/15 season. This is a photograph of the Toilet Department Ladies' Football Team for that period. The winners of the Ladies' Football League for the 1918 season were No. 1 Soapery team, and the runners up were No. 4 Soapery team.

PORT SUNLIGHT F.C.

Port Sunlight Football Club, 1933/4. Back row, left to right: J. Jones, W. Perry, W. Chetta, E. Richards, W. Weight, A. Bryan, J. Lund, P. Brown, S. Smart (referee). Front row: G. Ashton, W. Latters, D. Hughes, A. Tasker (captain), J. Storey, G. Thelwell. Originally members of the Liverpool Shipping League, this team were champions of the First Division 1926/7, runners up in 1927/8, and champions of the second division in 1931/2.

The Lever bus service. In June 1914 a service was established by Sir William Lever to run between Prenton tram terminus at the corner of Storeton Road/Prenton Road West and Raby, going via Thornton Hough. His aim was to provide some form of transport for the residents on the extensive Lever estates in the area. There were two buses, each seating between twenty and twenty-six passengers. The buses used several private roads on the Lever estate. Sir William had offered these roads to the Rural District Council, but they had declined, so the gates were kept locked and the conductor had to unlock and relock the gate each time the bus passed through.

In early September 1914, 700 male employees volunteered for the Army. After a farewell service in the Auditorium on Sunday 6 September, they departed the following morning, by train to Chester. Lever went with them and marched through the city. At Chester Castle they were enrolled in the 13th Battalion of the Cheshire Regiment.

The Battalion saw action in some of the bloodiest battles on the Western Front. Over 400 Lever Bros employees were killed, most of them from Port Sunlight. Because communities were losing all their young men in the same battles, group recruitment was stopped. The Standard of the 13th Cheshires hangs in Christ Church.

Another group of young men leaving Port Sunlight, marching to the railway station before proceeding to Chester to be enlisted. Their family and friends have turned out to bid them farewell.

This is part of the large crowd of local dignitaries, relatives, and employees of Lever Bros, at the unveiling of the First War Memorial on 3 December 1921. It was designed by Sir W. Goscombe John, its theme based on the 'defence of the home', and took from 1916 to 1921 to construct.

This postcard shows the body of Lord Leverhulme lying in state in the Lady Lever Art Gallery on 10 May 1925, flanked by a guard of honour, the Port Sunlight Works Fire Brigade. Here, his workers and friends could pay a last tribute before his burial alongside his wife in Christ Church.

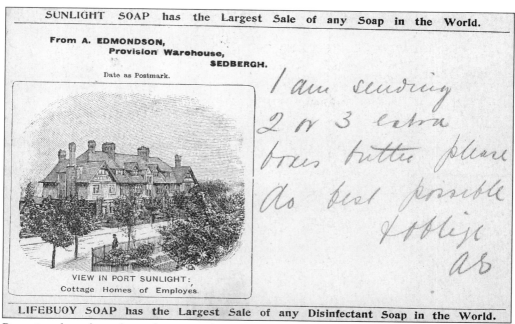

SUNLIGHT SOAP has the Largest Sale of any Soap in the World.

From A. EDMONDSON,
Provision Warehouse,
SEDBERGH.

Date as Postmark.

VIEW IN PORT SUNLIGHT:
Cottage Homes of Employes.

LIFEBUOY SOAP has the Largest Sale of any Disinfectant Soap in the World.

I am sending 2 or 3 extra boxes butter please do best possible & oblige A.E.

Pre-printed cards such as this one advertising the company's products were issued free to retailers for their correspondence. By sending out these cards they were also publicising Lever's products.

This was the type of horse-drawn transport used by Lever Bros in some areas in the 1880s. The three gentlemen in the picture are salesmen.

In 1900, one of the first motorised vehicles was this delivery wagon with its poster advertising Lifebuoy Carbolic Soap. Its disinfectant ingredients were included in the interests of good health.

This was one of a fleet of motor wagons used to deliver supplies throughout Wirral in 1904.

Six
Bromborough Pool and New Ferry

The New Ferry-Bromborough omnibus was very well patronised. A four-penny fare was money well spent to travel over that two-mile stretch, with never a house or a tree to break the monotony. The gentleman on the seat was Mr Jackson, who worked for Price's Patent Candle Works.

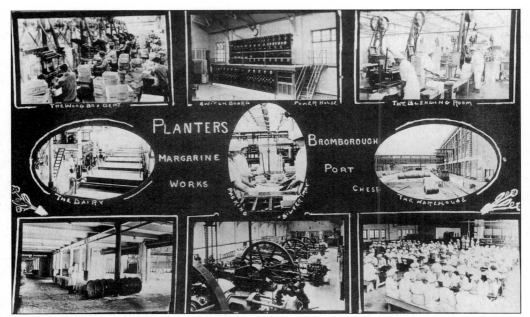

Planter's Margarine Works formed part of Lever Bros. This multi-view postcard shows various views of the works, and the process of manufacturing margarine.

Inside the Margarine Works in 1918. This was the box sealing department, where the finished products were enclosed in wooden boxes, labelled for their destinations, and prepared for the dispatch department.

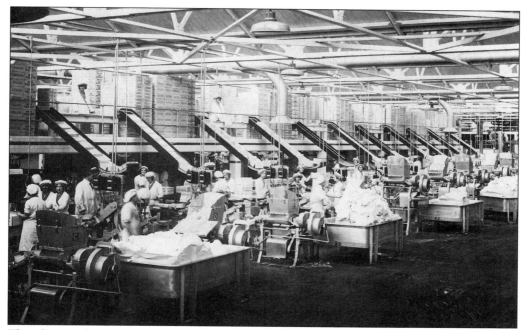

This shows a busy scene in the packing department in 1932. Most of the employees in this department are women.

These are some of the men who worked at Planter's Margarine Works in the 1930s. Famous brands soon became household names, such as Echo and Stork. Today, the works are known as the Stork Margarine Works.

Planter's Ladies Hockey Section, 1929/30. Back row, left to right: J.F.J. Nicholson (Honorary Secretary), J. Wood, H. Knight, L. Turner, L. Noonan, M. Wilkinson, M. Williamson, C. Bowe, N. Morris, B. Griffiths (Chairman). Middle row: M. Savidge, G. Ennion, D. Maybury, H. Dawson, I. Maybury, O. Warren, D. Noonan, G. Hough. Front row: E. Diamond, E. Curtis, I. Redmond, G. Smith (First Team Captain), E. Rogers, P. Walsh (Second Team Captain).

BROMBOROUGH MARGARINE R.U.F.C.

Planter's Bromborough Margarine Rugby Union Football Club. Back row, left to right: A. Sinclair (Honorary Secretary), J. Basnett (Committee), D. Campbell, G. Gill (Committee), H. McManus, T. Morley, J. Campbell, J. Hutcheon, J. Lewis, C. Hoole (Referee), H. Oughton (Chairman), W. Evans (Groundsman). Front row: L. Hopley, H. Daintith, A. Rowbotham, F. Robinson (Captain), B. Holmes, A. Ellison, J. Cummings, J. Gates. Sitting on the ground: W. Lally, A. Coathup. The club was formed in 1934, and was affiliated to Rugby Football Union and Cheshire County Union.

The Mersey in the grip of a severe winter. The building surrounded by the high wall is the Port of Liverpool Sanitary Isolation Hospital, built in 1875.

Prior to 1875 the quarantine station was a floating Lazarette which, for various reasons, was moved from place to place (for further reading on this subject see the author's *Looking Back at Maritime Wirral*).

The Isolation Hospital jetty meant that passengers and crews from infected ships could disembark straight into the hospital without coming into contact with any other person, thus preventing the spread of contagious diseases.

An icebound Bromborough Pool meant that none of the Price's barges could enter or leave Princes Dock, so sea transport came to a standstill.

In its early days, the entrance into Bromborough Pool was not protected. In the event of stormy weather, this meant that shipping moored there ran the risk of being severely battered.

A closer view of the shipwreck reveals it to be a barge belonging to Price's Patent Candle Company. In the background are the usual domed roofs of Price's Works. Their candle works in Battersea had roofs of a similar type.

This is the dock belonging to Price's Patent Candle Company, where their fleet of barges would unload their cargoes of vegetable oil, tallow, and other ingredients necessary for the making of candles, and then load up with the finished products for shipment to the ports of Birkenhead and Liverpool.

One of the fleet of barges that belonged to Price's Patent Candle Company in Bromborough Pool, *c.* 1870.

This is one of the many attractive posters that Prices Patent Candle Company used to promote their sales. The posters show that they made candles of all shapes and sizes, to suit every occasion.

The candlewick plaiting room in 1897. Cotton balls are placed in a drawer of the machine; a man takes the end of all the threads, doubles a portion of each end round a stick, and with a sharp blade cuts all the cottons to the proper length for the wick, giving the whole thing a slight twist with the machine before he removes them.

The 'New Patent' night light wicking room, 1897. It was a woman's job to insert the wicks in night lights. When lit, the candles were put to float in a saucer of water; at the end of the night, when the candle burnt down to water level, the water extinguished the flame.

Dip making room, 1897. Twenty candles hang on a broach. Thirty broaches are ranged side by side to form a frame; and thirty six frames are attached to a machine which dips them, one after the other, into the vessel of melted tallow.

From time to time the vessels of melted tallow require topping up. By this method, one man and his assistant can make thirty thousand candles a day.

Before Bromborough Docks were built in 1931, this lock could control the level in the tidal inlet Bromborough Pool.

Just after 4.00pm on 8 October 1940, a Junkers bomber flew in from the Irish Sea and upriver towards Ellesmere Port. After being damaged by anti-aircraft gunfire, it was attacked by three Hurricane fighters for a Czechoslovak squadron based at Speke. After an aerial battle the bomber crashed at Bromborough Dock. The late Councillor Harry Gill, a former Mayor of Bebington, accepted the surrender of the German aircraft crew who survived.

Bromborough Pool Lodge seen here in 1904 stood on the left-hand corner of the only road leading into Bromborough Pool Village. It is shown clearly on the 1930 Ordnance Survey Map, with the village War Memorial standing on the opposite corner.

The Cricket Club was founded in 1856, and in its heydey was able to play and often beat the best teams of Liverpool and district. The date of this team photograph is not known. Standing at the back: -?- Murray, S. Gratries, J. Lally, -?- Warburton, E. Davies. Middle row: G. Head, Harry ?, H. Eates, G. Wilson, W. Lavender. At the front: Joe Mercer, Tom ?, Jack Edwards.

York Street was the first group of houses to be built in 1854, the same year the village Ind. &
Provident Society was started. Here, at the corner of York Street, the village Co-op shop was
established.

Inside the busy village shop in Bromborough Pool, some time in the early 1950s.

After the foundation of the village, classes were held in one of the cottages and later in a works building known as the Iron House. Here, the teaching was done by the chaplain. When the first school was built in 1857, the headmistress was a Miss Humble, who had two lady assistants. When needed, the Assistant Works Manager was called in to administer corporal punishment.

On 16 January 1899 a new, larger school was opened, which accommodated 247 pupils. It was built of sandstone from the Company's nearby quarry and had adjoining playgrounds which were asphalted and partly covered. In 1902 this school was taken over by the Local Education Authority, and in 1931 it became a primary school for pupils up to eleven years of age. Both pictures are dated c. 1905.

One of the main events of the year's social calendar in Bromborough Pool Village was the annual sports day. Here is the tug-a-war event, a long pull and a strong pull. This sports day took place in 1907.

This is Bromborough Pool Football Club, 1907/8 season, when they were winners of the Zingari Cup.

142

Bromborough Pool Courthouse Farm was erected by the Hardware family, one member of which was twice Mayor of Chester. West of the house is the site where the Manor House belonging to the abbots of St Werbergs once stood. Notice the old New Ferry tram, used as an outbuilding.

Departing from the village of Bromborough Pool on the way to their summer camp at Meols in the year 1919 are boys of the local Church Lads Brigade Training Corps. The transport wagon belonged to Price's Patent Candle Works.

Weather permitting, the boys brought their personal equipment outside their tents every day and laid it out for inspection.

At the end of the camping period, an official photograph was taken of the entire group before they departed for home. The chaplain appears to be looking down at some fidgety boy.

Looking towards the new bridge being constructed over Bromborough Pool and the River Dibbin on the New Chester Road in 1932. The previous one had lasted since the days when the road had been built as a turnpike. (Photograph by Stan Evans)

This is how the New Chester Road bridge looked when it was completed, with the river traffic proceeding unhindered. The whole of this area is now being filled in.

Pupils of New Chester Road Council School at New Ferry in 1928. Identified in the front row are: Tom Linson, -?- Richards, -?- Pratt, -?- Greaves. Second row: T. Hew, -?- Glover, -?- Hatton. Third row: -?- Mason, -?- Beveridge, -?- Mitchell. Back row: -?- Jennings, T. Williams, -?- Pritchard. The teacher was Mr J. Nichols.

The New Chester Road was not freed from tolls until 1883. The butcher shop of John Edge, shown here at New Ferry Toll Bar, is still here under the ownership of the same family; the boy in the shandry was the present owner's father, and the man with the tall hat was his grandfather.

This is one of the original horse-drawn tram cars bought in 1877, pictured outside the depot in New Ferry. The Wirral Tramway Company's line ran from Woodside and along the New Chester Road to the Toll Bar at New Ferry, where the cars terminated outside the company's depot. It is believed that the young boys in uniform may have been employees, their job being to change the horses when required.

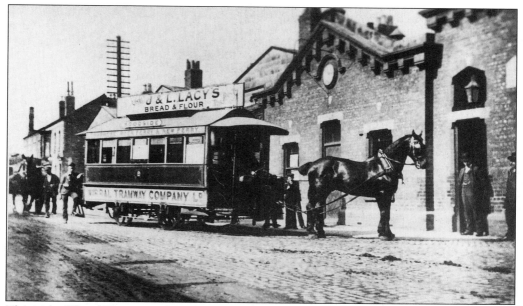

This is the Wirral Tramways Company car no. 9 outside the New Ferry depot about 1890. This type of car was known as a turtle back, because of the shape of its roof. The last Wirral company horse tram ran on the evening of 8 May 1900, and was met by a crowd because of fog signals at New Ferry (see page 156).

New Ferry   Old Toll Bar Corner

Because the country was in mourning following the death of Queen Victoria, the single-deck electric service started at 5.30am on 4 February 1901 without pomp and ceremony.

Both the horse tram and the single deck electric tram were designed to this height because of the low railway bridge in Chester Street, Birkenhead. The bridge carried the LNW/GW railway branch to Abbey Street coal sidings, and Laird's shipyards.

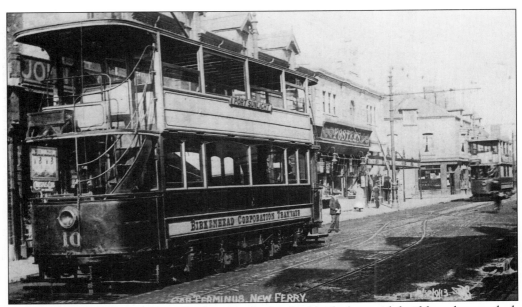

The single-deck cars were later rebuilt as low-bridge double-deckers with knifeboard upper deck seating. There were paired seats back to back the length of the car, with the foot rests above the heads of the downstairs passengers. The overhead cables under the bridge had to be carefully arranged to locate with the specially sprung trolley poles.

The *Royal George* was one of seven named buses in the Crosville fleet before the First World War. Some of the other names were *Alma*, *Deva*, *Flying Fox*, and *Busy Bee*. It was new in 1912 and had an open rear platform. It operated between Chester and New Ferry, travelling via Ellesmere Port.

The *Royal George*, seen here leaving the New Ferry Toll Bar on the first day of the New Ferry to Chester service, on 25 January 1913.

The New Ferry Toll Bar symbolised the Great Divide between Birkenhead public transport and Crosville which was in existence until 1930.

On the left is tram no. 8, originally a single decker. On the right is Crosville GH7 which dates from 1924 and which in this photograph had just left the company's bus station (see opposite).

These were the days when a policeman controlled the busy Toll Bar crossroads. There is a clear view down Ferry Road.

This was Crosville's combined bus station and garage in New Ferry Road, near the Toll Bar, *c.* 1928. The Leyland Leviathan No. 220 was on the Bromborough local service. The depot was used until March 1932 and was later converted to a market.

It is the early 1900s, and the streets are bustling with people waiting for the street parade during New Ferry carnival.

During their visit to Port Sunlight on 25 March 1914, King George V and Queen Mary paid a brief visit to New Ferry. In the background is the Post Office and the business premises of J.G. Davies (see page 159).

New Chester Road, in the early 1920s. The film advertised as being shown at the Lyceum was *The Light of Western Stars* starring Jack Holt & Noah Berry, a silent movie made in 1925. (Collection of the late Revd Jim McTear)

Further down the road, at about the same time. (Collection of the late Revd Jim McTear)

Part of the long road that stretched down to the ferry. In the distance can be seen the cupola on the roof of the Ferry Hotel, once a prominent landmark, and now gone.

When steamers were not sailing from New Ferry because of fog, two white lights, attached to tramway standards between New Ferry and St. Paul's Church, were switched on. Fog tickets gave regular passengers free travel to and from Woodside on the trams.

Rock Ferry may have had its own private park, but New Ferry still has its very own private promenade which is available only to tenants and friends.

The boat on the foreshore belonged to one of the training ships moored in the background, and was used to fetch the boys ashore. They had a sports field not far away, complete with its own pavilion.

Of the three wooden warships, this was the nearest to New Ferry. Originally known as the *Indie*, she was built in 1848 and was replaced at her station here in 1914 by the ship opposite.

This is the second *Indefatigable*, an iron ship which was here until 1941. Her original name was *Phaeton*.

This is a photograph of the late J. George Davies, the local photographer who recorded many local scenes and events on postcards – many of which appear in this book. His son later took over the business. The shop can be seen in the royal visit picture shown on page 154.

Acknowledgements

Compiling this book has only been been achieved with the help and generosity of the many people who have lent me photographs, postcards, and who have shared their knowledge and expertise. I wish to thank the following:

The late Mrs A. Anderson, Mr I. Boumphrey, Mr M. Day, Mr J. Dibdin, Mr. T. Gerry, Mr R. Hignett, Mrs J. Howard and her daughter Louise, Mrs J. Hyde, Mrs G. Jackson, Mr & Mrs J. Martin, Mrs J. Moore, Senior Assistant, Information Services, Bebington Library, Miss S. and Mr B. Nicholson, Mr M. Roberts, Mr J. Ryan, Mr L. Smith, Mr T. Turner, Mr G. Weaver, Mr R. Wilson.

In addition to the above my special thanks for invaluable help go to the following: Mr Bill Norton, Principal Librarian of Bibliographical and Computer Services, Wirral Libraries; Miss Karen Duncan, Information Officer at Port Sunlight Heritage Centre; Lever Bros. & Port Sunlight Heritage for permission to use material from their collections; Mr T.B. Maund, transport historian and author; Mike Lister; Glyn Parry; Jeffrey Pearson, Creative Photography, Wallasey; The Bromborough Society; Mary, Carol and staff at Max Spielman's. I apologise to anyone that I may have omitted.

I dedicate this book to my wife, Norah Rowena,
and to all those above who made it possible.